Usborne First Experiences
Going to the Dentist

Anne Civardi

Illustrated by Stephen Cartwright

Edited by Michelle Bates

Cover design by Neil Francis

There is a little yellow duck hiding on every double page. Can you find it?

This is the Judd family.

Mr. Judd

Mrs. Judd

Jake Judd

Jessie Judd

Jasper

Jake and Jessie need to have a check-up with their dentist.
Mr. Judd phones to make an appointment.

A few days later, they go to see the dentist.

Mrs. Judd takes Jake and Jessie in her car. Mr. Judd stays at home with Jasper the dog.

The dentist is very busy.

There are lots of people waiting to see him. Jake and Jessie play in the waiting room until it is their turn.

Jake and Jessie meet the dental assistant.

She calls them in to see the dentist. She is going to help with Jake and Jessie's check-up.

"Hello Jake, hello Jessie," says the dentist.

"Hello," say Jake and Jessie. The dentist says that Mrs. Judd can come in and watch.

Jessie goes first.

Jessie sits in a special chair that can go up and down.
Then the dental assistant puts a bib around Jessie's neck.

Jessie has her teeth checked.

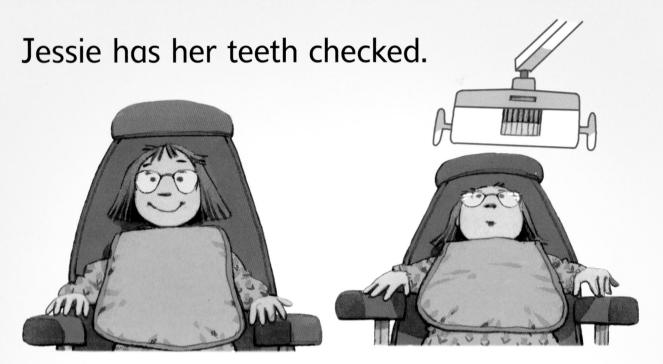

There is a spotlight above Jessie that shines into her mouth.

The dentist wears special gloves and a mask over his nose and mouth. He puts the chair back before he checks Jessie's teeth.

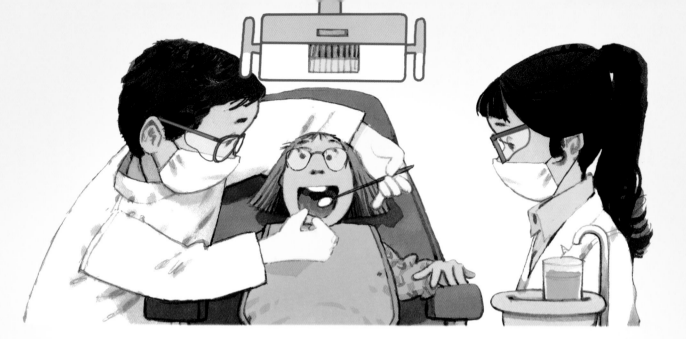

Jessie opens her mouth wide. He uses a mirror to see inside.

The dentist looks at each of Jessie's teeth. The dental assistant makes notes about them on the computer.

The dentist has finished with Jessie.

He is very pleased with her. Jessie has no holes in her
teeth. Now she can rinse out her mouth.

Now it is Jake's turn.

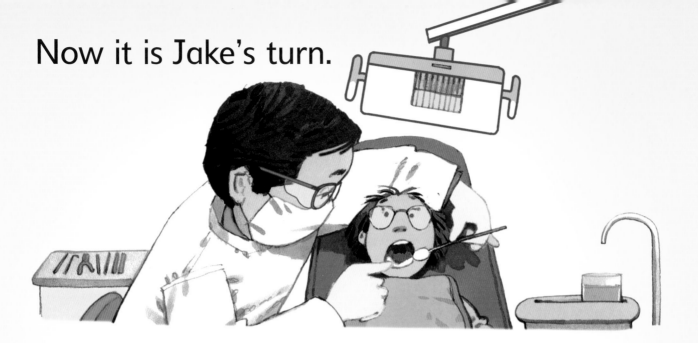

When the dentist checks Jake's teeth he finds a small hole in one of them. This means that Jake needs to have a filling.

The dentist rubs some gel onto Jake's gums and makes Jake's tooth numb.

Jake has a filling.

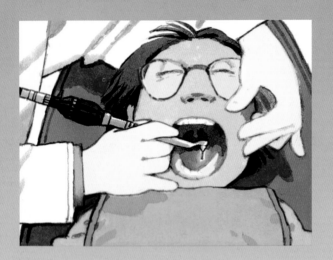 

The dentist removes the bad part of Jake's tooth. A suction hose is used to keep Jake's mouth dry.

Then the filling materials are prepared for the dentist.

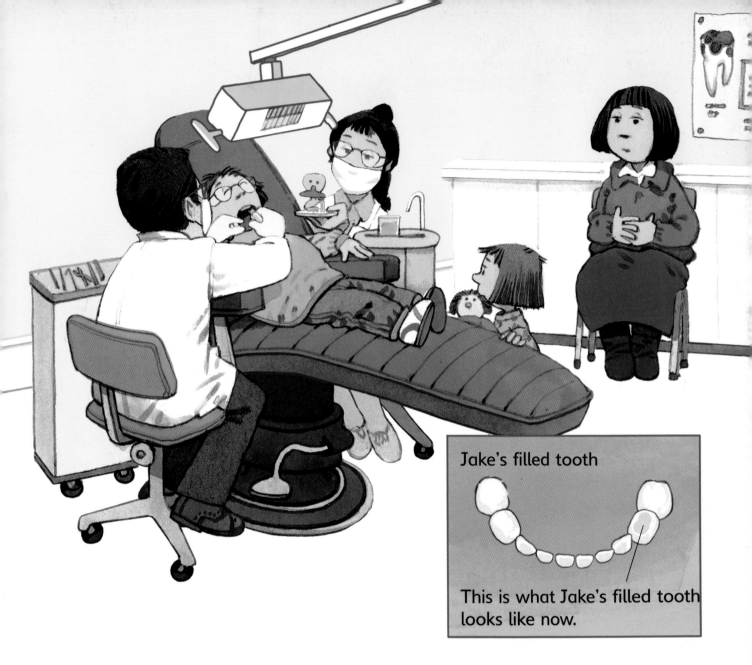

Jake's filled tooth

This is what Jake's filled tooth looks like now.

The dentist puts the filling in place. Now Jake will not get a toothache.

The children learn to take care of their teeth.

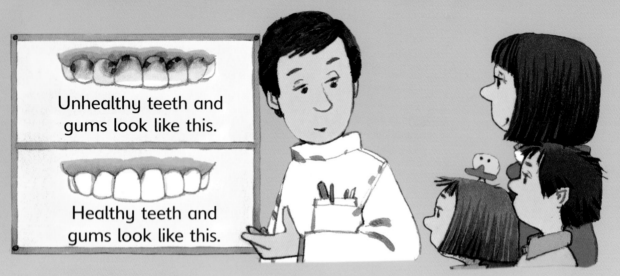

Unhealthy teeth and gums look like this.

Healthy teeth and gums look like this.

The dentist shows them what will happen if they don't take care of their teeth properly.

Eat more of these.

Eat less of these.

He says they should be careful what they eat and drink because sugar and sweet foods and drinks are bad for teeth.

Jake and Jessie learn how to brush and floss their teeth really well. This gets rid of old food that can cause holes.

Jake and Jessie must brush their teeth twice a day with fluoride toothpaste to keep them clean and healthy.

Jake and Jessie go home.

On their way out, Mrs. Judd makes an appointment to see the dentist for another check-up in six months.

This edition published in 2009 by Usborne Publishing Ltd, Usborne House, 83-85 Saffron Hill, London ECIN 8RT, England.
Revised and updated in 2009. Copyright © 2009, 2005, 1992 Usborne Publishing Ltd. www.usborne.com
The name Usborne and the devices ♀♀ are Trade Marks of Usborne Publishing Ltd. All rights reserved. No part of this
publication may be reproduced, stored in a retrieval system, or transmitted in any form or by any means electronic, mechanical,
photocopying, recording or otherwise, without prior permission of the publisher. AE. This edition first published in America in 2009.